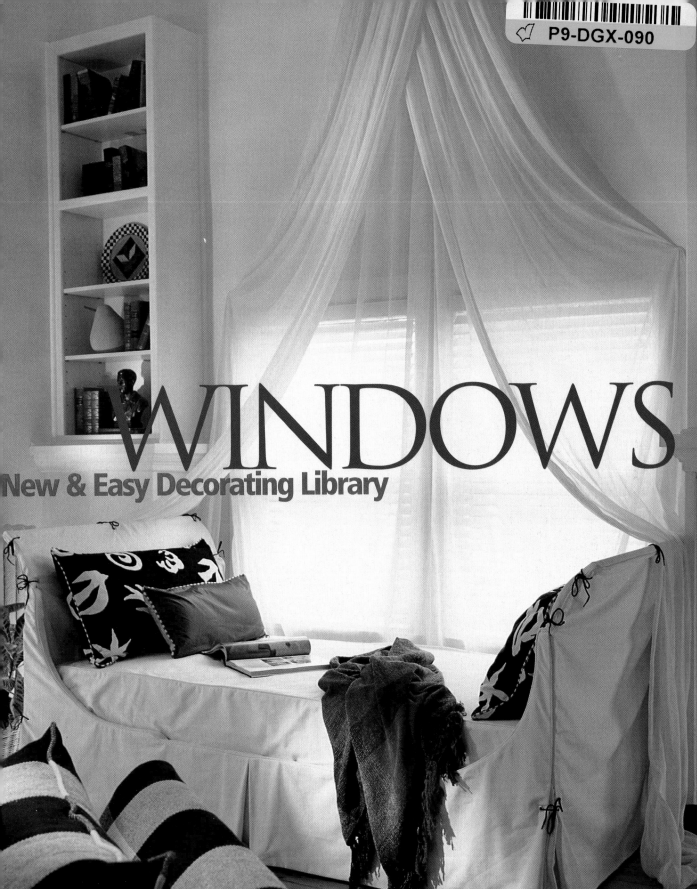

WINDOWS
New & Easy Decorating Library

BETTER HOMES AND GARDENS® BOOKS
Des Moines, Iowa

New & Easy Decorating Library
Better Homes and Gardens® Books An imprint of Meredith® Books
Published for Creative World Enterprises LP, West Chester, Pennsylvania
www.1CreativeWorld.com

WINDOWS Volume 4
Project Editors: Denise L. Caringer, Linda Hallam
Art Director: Jerry J. Rank
Copy Chief: Catherine Hamrick
Copy and Production Editor: Terri Fredrickson
Contributing Copy Editor: Margaret Smith
Contributing Proofreaders: Kathy Eastman, Colleen Johnson, Gretchen Kauffman
Electronic Production Coordinator: Paula Forest
Editorial and Design Assistants: Kaye Chabot, Mary Lee Gavin, Karen Schirm
Production Director: Douglas M. Johnston
Production Managers: Pam Kvitne, Marjorie J. Schenkelberg

Meredith® Books
Editor in Chief: James D. Blume
Design Director: Matt Strelecki
Managing Editor: Gregory H. Kayko

Director, Sales & Marketing, Retail: Michael A. Peterson
Director, Sales & Marketing, Special Markets: Rita McMullen
Director, Sales & Marketing, Home & Garden Center Channel: Ray Wolf
Director, Operations: George A. Susral

Vice President, General Manager: Jamie L. Martin

***Better Homes and Gardens*® Magazine**
Editor in Chief: Jean LemMon
Executive Interior Design Editor: Sandra S. Soria

Meredith Publishing Group
President, Publishing Group: Christopher M. Little
Vice President, Consumer Marketing & Development: Hal Oringer

Meredith Corporation
Chairman and Chief Executive Officer: William T. Kerr

Chairman of the Executive Committee: E. T. Meredith III

Creative World Enterprises LP
Publisher: Richard J. Petrone
Design Consultants to Creative World Enterprises: Coastline Studios, Orlando, Florida

All of us at Better Homes and Gardens® Books are dedicated to providing you with information and ideas to enhance your home. We welcome your comments and suggestions. Write to us at: Better Homes and Gardens Books, Shelter Editorial Department, 1716 Locust St., Des Moines, IA 50309-3023.

If you would like to purchase any of our books, check wherever quality books are sold. Visit our website at bhg.com or bhgbooks.com.

CONTENTS
New & Easy Decorating For Windows

Windows are the eyes of your home. The treatments you use to frame those eyes affect how you view the world outside—as well as your world inside. Window treatments are more than a finishing touch: They lend importance to ordinary windows, provide privacy, and filter sunlight. Use your windows to explore your creativity and sense of personal style.

More than any other element, windows define your home's architecture. They come in many shapes and styles—often in the same house. Some are tall,

Getting STARTED

graceful, and topped by an arch; others may be small and awkward beneath the eaves of an attic. The right window treatment enhances a beautiful room, takes a cheerless space and makes it a sanctuary, or contributes to sun, temperature, or privacy. Sometimes the window is such a strong element that it stands alone or with minimal treatment. More often, the right treatment transforms plain, nondescript windows into decorating assets for your home. When you consider that the average home has between 20 and 30 windows, that's a great opportunity to put your creativity into practice.

Plan your window treatments when you choose wall colors, furnishings, and floor coverings so everything works together. As you begin, consider the type of room, the function and type of the windows in the room, the decor of the room as well as your home, and your budget. Ask yourself whether you want windows to be a focal point or a backdrop. How much natural light do you want? In a room with many windows facing south, for instance, choose adjustable shutters or miniblinds that fend off the sun without blocking light.

Make a statement of your personal style with window treatments. There are no hard and fast rules as to which treatments go with particular styles of furnishings. In fact, depending upon how bold you feel, you may want to pair opposites for drama, such as teaming contemporary window treatments with a traditional room style. Whatever your decision, window treatments contribute to the tone and feel of your rooms. Classic tailored swags and floor-puddling panels speak of tradition; perky curtains enhance casual, cottage, and country looks. Balloon shades and soft valances create a romantic backdrop for pretty fabrics and furnishings. Sleek fabric shades, blinds, and shutters control light and privacy in rooms with contemporary flair.

Dress a window in a long, lush drapery, and it's as though a woman put on an evening gown—instant glamour. As with dresses, certain factors determine the formality of the drapery. Consider fabric type and pattern—silk damask, for example, is much more formal than a cotton check. Silk may work beautifully dressing the windows in a formal dining room, but will be sorely out of place in a casual family room. Elaborate headers and complex construction also denote formality. Generally, longer curtains are more formal than shorter ones.

Draperies & CURTAINS

Evoke farmhouse charm with blissfully simple curtains that make no pretense at grandeur. Look for hardy fabrics, such as cottons or linens, in room-friendly prints—checks, florals, stripes, or plaids. Keep the heading as plain as possible. Tabs top most classic casual curtains (especially country curtains), but wood rings on a rod are equally informal. Above all, keep embellishments to a minimum.

That doesn't mean unpretentious curtains can't catch the eye. Set brightly hued draperies against a white backdrop, pair patterned curtains with complementary wallpaper, or team colored draperies with contrasting walls to make sure they get noticed. Repeat the curtain fabric as accents on pillows or chairs.

DRAPERIES & CURTAINS

Detail with paint. A hand-painted daffodil design on the narrow cornice accentuates the yellow-and-white scheme, *below*. These cornices also hide the drapery hardware of the window treatment so that the curtain looks free-floating. The drapery consists of stationary box-pleated panels with pinch-pleat panels beneath. The combination works well, as it cuts sunlight and allows privacy on the lower window, while exposing and calling attention to the lovely curves of the upper fanlight.

Keep it casual. Green plaid panels in a cotton-linen blend bring no-fuss simplicity to formal windows, *opposite*. Hung below the arches to avoid concealing dramatic window details, this lined treatment admits sunlight while protecting privacy. The black iron rods, curtain rings, and fleur-de-lis finials contribute to the casual effect. Plus, they pull out the black from the plaid fabric for a visually connected look that unifies the overall decorating scheme. Message: This is a room for relaxing.

DRAPERIES & CURTAINS

Trim unlined burlap. Pair the rugged and the refined with velvet-trimmed, unlined drapery panels hung from decorative iron rods. This cost-conscious look imparts sophistication to a living or dining room of eclectic furnishings.

DRAPERIES & CURTAINS

Hardware counts. Until recently, window hardware remained in the background—the hardworking support staff for draperies and curtains—hardly a player in its own right. That's changed, and all for the best. Rods are wood, iron, brass, or even clear acrylic, allowing you to create an endless number of styles. Finials are also available in a wide variety of materials and motifs. Decide first whether you want the hardware to fade into the background or become an important design element, as the window, *opposite*, attests. Note the pairing of the black hardware, including tiebacks and rings, with the dressy sheers.

Feature fuller fabrics. Go with the luxury of yardage rather than costly fabric. Hang unlined, light-diffusing cotton from wrought iron S-hooks. Use rubber O-rings to creatively and softly gather the fabric. Notice how the draperies, *right*, hang just beneath the crown molding and puddle gently on the floor for a graceful effect. When two rooms open to each other, repeat the window treatment to avoid distraction.

DRAPERIES & CURTAINS

Cloth tab curtains. Use ribbons to transform cotton tab curtains into spectacular curtains, *below*. First, cut off the original ties. Stitch ribbons along the outer edges of the fabric and in place of the ties, extending them the full length of the curtains. Though the ribbon shown here yielded a fresh, feminine style, the design possibilities are unlimited.

A quick change of mood. For a temporary window dressing, drape a colorful vintage or lace tablecloth in the window, *above right*. It couldn't be easier—a tension rod is the trick. Just fold a tablecloth in half diagonally, center the rod along the fold, and pull the tablecloth around the rod once. Place the rod in the window, adjusting and smoothing as needed.

Who says fast and easy can't be clever, too? Have some fun with window treatments in the kitchen or bath. Use cotton tea towels to replicate the look of Grandma's clothesline, *opposite*. Use an awl or a drill to make pilot holes. Install wooden drawer pulls to hold the clothesline in place. Tie the rope to the drawer pulls, allowing it to sag in the center. Attach towels to the rope with clothespins.

DRAPERIES & CURTAINS

OFF-THE-RACK STYLE
Start with ready-made curtains, then add your own special touches.
• *Instant valances.* Toss a folded tablecloth, lace panel, or even a favorite scarf over the rod.
• *Contrasting tiebacks.* Loop long, straight curtain panels over collectible antique doorknobs screwed into the walls at the desired height. Or, replace matching fabric tiebacks with decorative ribbon, yarn, raffia, or contrasting fabric strips (perhaps braided together).
• *Decorative rods.* Basic curtains take on newfound style when teamed with decorative rods and finials from stores, catalogs, salvage shops, or even nature (as in sturdy twigs).

No longer lonely at the top. Handsome rods keep company with decorative tabs and other curtain-top treatments. Custom sheer panels hang by spaghetti straps over a gracefully shaped, hand-forged iron rod, *above.* The black iron bed and tiebacks balance the rod's visual weight. The rugged beauty of the rod contrasts with the ethereal curtains.

Swing wide. When hinged rods open, *opposite,* curtains disappear against the walls. For privacy at night, they swing shut. From a maintenance standpoint, there is nothing easier—no pulling or tying required. Home decorating and window covering catalogs carry these adjustable specialty rods.

Cornices and valances are the window treatments that bring out the fun and creativity in home decorators. Don't let their small size fool you: These top treatments pack decorating punch. Use them alone when privacy isn't a factor; combine them with shades or blinds when it is. Paired with operable or fixed drapery panels, they create a luxurious look, *opposite.* Cornices are usually stiff, made of fabric-covered wood; valances are soft, made of fabric. Rigid cornices suggest greater formality than fluid valances; however, every rule has its

Cornices & VALANCES

exceptions. Many children's rooms have decorative, painted cornices that are pure flights of fancy. And softly draped valances grace formal living and dining rooms. **The variety and hanging techniques of valances convey limitless** moods and styles. A loosely hung valance imparts a casual look; a more tailored valance suggests formality. Tie tabs to a wooden rod for farmhouse appeal or drape a window scarf over a rod. As another choice, eyebrow folds are easy to make. Cut a rectangle of fabric, line and hem it, fold it accordion style, and hang it from two hooks. Experiment with these and other methods for a look you like.

CORNICES & VALANCES

Light-touch windows. Trimmed sheers, *opposite,* give this gathering of Scandinavian country pieces an air of formality. Sheers cleverly mimic the forms of traditional swagged valances and drapery side panels while allowing light to bathe the living room. Unlike the plain white sheers from the past, new colors and patterns are available. The striped valance sheer adds a hint of pattern that doesn't compete with the other prints in the room.

A layered window treatment. Valances over sheer side panels and wood blinds, *above,* provide this living room privacy and a romantic contemporary look. Pale walls are intentionally understated. The valance introduces scallop curves to soften the space. Dressmaker details such as knotted corners and gold fringed edges add formality and fun. Despite the clever good looks, sheers don't shield the sun: Blinds do that job.

CORNICES & VALANCES

More than a topper. Consider a lambrequin, a short, decorative-shaped cornice, often with extended sides, *below*. Such detailed cornices usually are traced or drawn onto plywood, then cut with a jigsaw. Choose a design with motifs and trim that enhance your room decor.

Window as focal point. A star-painted valance with gilded wood ornaments maximizes the celestial theme, *opposite*. Trim fabric from a valance works well for additional accents, such as this window-seat cushion. To construct such an unusually shaped valance, measure the window first and cut a full-size pattern from kraft paper. Line and hang snugly for the most pleasing effect.

CORNICES & VALANCES

Rich country French toile.
This home office has an Old World ambience that is anything but cold and high-tech. But too much of a good thing isn't good: Creamy draperies break up the busy wall pattern, and cornices topped with crown molding lend height and vintage style to modern windows while maintaining simplicity.

CORNICES & VALANCES

Create a fashionable scalloped valance. Hang gathered rose-and-white stripe fabric from an iron rod with movable clips, available from home furnishings stores and catalogs, *above left*. Use small finials in a classic motif for this French-inspired look that adds romance and charm to an old-fashioned bedroom.

Hang a cornice. Installed at or above the window frame, *above center,* this eye-catching treatment avoids competition with the casing trim. If you plan to use blinds or a roller shade, make sure the decorative cornice is hung deep enough inside the frame to conceal the necessary hardware.

Balloon or cornice. Is it a cornice or is it a valance? Only its permanence can determine for sure. In this example, fabric is permanently affixed to the wall to fill the function of a cornice, *above right*. The sporty check fabric, ruffled at the top and sides and ballooned at the bottom, visually lengthens a low ceiling. Hung at ceiling height and extending only a third of the way down the window, the window treatment also maximizes the amount of sunlight. Add sheers for diffused light; use shades or blinds if more privacy is needed.

CORNICES & VALANCES

Decorate with a stylish, shaped cornice treatment. Choose a shape and design that make the most of a designer print fabric, *opposite*. The same fabric repeats as the trim to a bed canopy, constructed of a less expensive, solid cotton. Shop crafts stores for wood ornaments that can be painted or gilded to trim such inventive treatments.

Create your cornice. Use kits available at fabric stores to create the border, *right*. Following the kit instructions, cut foam pieces to fit the window. Select fabrics and trims to decorate. To cover, cut polyester quilt batting (medium loft) 6 inches larger than the cornice on all sides. Cut the fabric the same size. Using pins, a hot-glue gun, or fabric glue, attach the batting to the cornice. Wrap the batting to the back of the cornice and pin or glue in place. Wrap the fabric around the cornice and batting, folding for smooth edges. Pin or glue in place. For a finished look, pin or glue cording along the upper and lower edges.

POINTED PLEASURE

For this easy topper, *left,* the fabric itself forms the cornice. You'll need only to cut a 3-inch-deep board that is as wide as your window. Cut out fabric to form the face and ends, adding ½ inch to all edges for seams. Cut a fabric lining the same size. Sew the lining to the fabric, with right sides together, leaving an opening for turning right side out. Trim seams, clip corners, turn, and press. Slip-stitch the opening closed. Sew or glue fringe to the lower edge. Center fabric on the board, smoothing front-facing fabric over the top of the board, and staple. Fold the end fabric gift-wrap style over the top for smooth corners. Glue cording to the top edge and fringed trim to the bottom. Mount the board to the window trim with screws or to the wall above the window using L-brackets.

Curtains get the glory, but shades combine pragmatism with style. Balloon and Roman shades minimize fabric and contribute pattern, color, and softness without stealing the show. Hard treatments—blinds and pleated shades—solve window issues from privacy to architectural awkwardness. Both work with or in place of draperies or where flowing fabrics are impractical. Handsome and timeless, shutters are a classic decorating element. While offering some protection against heat and cold, they don't completely

Blinds, Shutters, & SHADES

block light; they diffuse and soften it for a romantic ambience.

Shutter slats are more than an engineering element; they convey style. Stir up a breezy tropical mood with wide-slat plantation shutters, create a cottage atmosphere with small-slat cafe shutters, or produce a farmhouse air with solid shutters. All are painted or stained in a range of colors.

The downside to shutters? Cost. Depending on size and style, custom-ordered shutters can be the priciest of all permanent window treatments. There's an additional precaution: Think twice before using shutters in a space already busy with linear design and strong architecture.

Swag-and-jabot combined. This softly tailored treatment frames the window, *below*, with classic formality. It consists of three pieces: a draped swag and two pleated sides—the jabots or tails. Fabric stores offer swag-and-jabot patterns in several styles, or be bold and make your own pattern.

Shade of difference. A solid or damask-weave translates best into this shade in which the design creates the interest, *opposite*. Choose lightweight fabric that softly filters but does not totally block natural light. Measure the inner window width and add 1 inch. Measure the length of window and add 2¼ inches. Cut fabric to those dimensions. At the bottom edge of the fabric, cut a soft curve.

BLINDS, SHUTTERS, & SHADES

Budget-conscious style. Pair stylish bamboo-finish matchstick blinds with floor-length sheer panels on a decorative rod for a tropical atmosphere, *opposite*. Then sit back and enjoy the light show. Both the blinds and sheers play with sunlight, casting interesting shadows and dappling surfaces. The light window treatment balances heavier elements, such as the sofa and coffee table.

Think narrow-slat. Install natural wood blinds, *above left,* when diffused light, not sun control, is your objective. Natural wood warms any room, so use wood blinds to remove a chill. Or, use them in the presence of other warm woods for a masculine, denlike effect.

Custom-crafted in print fabric. A problem-solving roller shade, *above right,* pairs with handsome trimmed draperies in a frankly formal living room. The pluses of this handsome twosome are sunlight control and insulation with the bonus of a contrasting decorative textile.

One room two ways: Try scarves. For a quick-and-easy, affordable, and stylish treatment, the beauty of window dressing with scarves is twofold: draping ability and pre-finish, *above*. Already cut and hemmed, scarves are ready to display. Get the effect you want by swirling the scarf over a curtain rod. Team the beauty of a soft scarf with the privacy of a wheat-color woven shade for an unbeatable combination that's both good-looking and hard-working. Tip: To add length, stitch dresser or apparel scarves together at the narrow ends.

One room two ways: Go sheer. A chic window dressing enhances this clean-cut, contemporary living room, *above*. A single, long bolt of sheer fabric is draped over both ends of a decorative iron rod to fall loosely as side panels. The advantage of this treatment is a liberated fuss-free look—no measuring to size required. A touch of fringe enhances the appeal of the fabric, and a woven shade ensures privacy. Tip: Before ordering shades, measure every window—though they may all look the same, there may be slight variations in size.

BLINDS, SHUTTERS, & SHADES

CURTAIN CALL

■ Hot sun? No view?
Treat your eyes to a
cheery fabric instead of
blinding rays. Line a
tightly woven fabric,
such as this cotton
chintz, *left,* and attach it
with a tension rod inside
the window frame. Tack
contrasting ribbon in
place to gently pull up
and swag the fabric.

■ Nothing destroys
fabrics faster than the
sun. If you live in a sunny
climate, opt for an acrylic
fabric that won't
succumb to sun damage.
Light-color fabrics
generally reflect sunlight
and resist fading. Dark
colors absorb light and
will fade. For the best
sun protection, line
window treatments and
back them with a blind
or shade to cut the rays.

Neat in appearance. Roman shades work well in bathrooms, kitchens, and children's rooms, where
an elaborate fabric treatment might overwhelm. In this stylish master bathroom with a coastal decor, a
wide Roman shade with a seashell motif covers a pair of windows, *opposite.* Mount the shade inside
or outside the window frame. Outside mounts offer the most in insulation and blocking light, and
inside mounts show off more window frame. To cut costs, use a commercial pattern to sew your own
or order standard size Roman shades from a curtain catalog. Some national discount stores sell fabric
Roman shades. Measure the windows carefully when you order or purchase a Roman shade. Tip: Detail
a stock Roman shade with trim for your own customized look.

Enjoy privacy. Admit light with a shade that's sheer at the top and opaque at the bottom, *below*. To raise the shade, roll it from the bottom, and secure it at the desired height with pretty ribbon ties. The double fold of fabric softens light and frames the view.

Polar Attraction. Stitch a shade from a Polarfleece throw, *opposite*:

1. For the sides, cut two pieces one-third the window width and the same height as the window, plus 2 inches. Be sure each edge has edging.

2. For the center, cut one piece one-third the window width, plus 2 inches, and the same height as the window, plus 2 inches. With right sides facing and edges even, stitch pieces together so the edging falls on either side. Trim and iron.

3. Cut two pieces of twill tape one-half the shade length. Turn top edges of tape under and align with shade top. Position tape on shade front to cover seam lines; turn bottom edges of tape under. Pin and stitch.

4. For shade back, cut two pieces of twill tape one-half the shade length, plus 8 inches. Sew along the same stitching lines, leaving the first 8 inches unstitched. Turn loose ends of tape under twice and topstitch.

5. Stitch decorative buttons along front tapes. Add buttonholes to ends of tapes; roll up and button in place.

If you've decided to tackle your window treatments yourself, follow the advice of design experts for a professional look you'll be proud to claim.

Include a lining to avoid a cut-and-sew pattern look. Use heavy fleece to give lasting body. Depending on the style, interline between the fabric and the lining.

Flimsiness spells homemade. Select a complementary fabric for contrasting draperies, swags and jabots, and shades.

Deck your dressing with trims, such as welting, fringe, braids, and tassels, for a custom finish. Highlight the bottom edge of the drape with contrasting welting. Buy commercial patterns with instructions on sewing and adding trims to your treatments.

Help draw draperies hang smoothly by sewing drapery weights (available at fabric stores) into the hems.

Keep dressings full, even if it means buying two panels and sewing them together.

The key to sewing window treatments yourself or buying ready-made ones is learning how to measure your windows accurately. It's especially important if you order blinds and other shades yourself. They are custom-made for your windows, and they aren't returnable.

1. Use a steel measuring tape. Decide whether you want your treatments to fit inside your window (an inside mount is the most common) or to cover your window (an outside mount). Measure accurately.

2. For an inside mount, measure the opening width at the top, middle, and bottom, recording the narrowest measurement. Do the same for the length, recording the longest measurement. Round to the closest ⅛ inch.

3. For an outside mount, measure the opening width and add at least 3 inches to each side of the window opening if there is room. Measure the opening length and add at least 2 inches in height for hardware and any overlap.

4. To measure the drop for draperies, measure the windows from where you intend to install the rod to where you want draperies to fall. For width, measure full length of the rod. To calculate the length of a decorative scarf or a single fabric piece, measure the distance from the bottom of the drapery ring or the top of the rod to the desired length of the scarf. Multiply that measurement by 2 and add 10 inches to each side if you want the fabric to puddle on the floor. Measure width of the area to be covered and add that figure to the length for the total yardage needed.

Sheets are a do-it-yourself dream. Relatively inexpensive and readily available, sheets can be made into many styles of soft window dressing. Shop outlets for seconds or look for sales to get the best buys. To make these curtains yourself:

1. Measure your window, then choose a sheet about twice the width of the window. Plan for two sheets per window.

2. Determine the length of your panels. For a ruffled header, you'll need a sheet that is 8 to 12 inches longer than your desired finished length.

3. To make one panel, lay out a flat sheet right side up. Measure down from the top edge 8 to 12 inches or more, depending on the desired fullness of your header. Bring the top edge of the sheet back up to about 1 inch above the fold. Fold this 1-inch margin to the back side of the sheet.

4. Topstitch along the edge of the panel, catching all layers.

5. Sew rings along the top edge.

QUICK TIPS ON SEWING